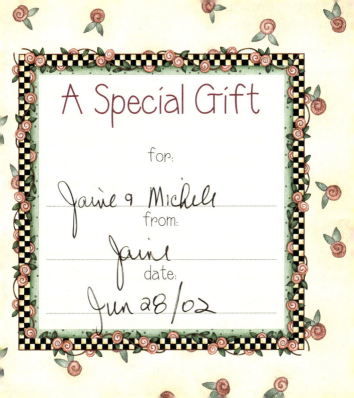

A Special Gift

for:

Jamie & Michele

from:

Jamie

date:

Jun 28/02

75 Things To Do
With a Friend

Written by
Conover Swofford

Illustrated by

DebbieMumm

Brownlow

Little Treasures Miniature Books

75 Things to do With a Friend

75 Ways to Be Good to Yourself

75 Ways to Calm Your Soul

75 Ways to Spoil Your Grandchild

A Little Book of Blessing

A Little Book of Love

A Little Book for Tea Lovers

A Roof with a View

Baby's First Little Book

Baby Love

Baby Oh Baby

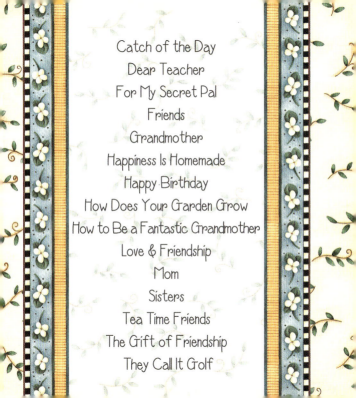

Catch of the Day

Dear Teacher

For My Secret Pal

Friends

Grandmother

Happiness Is Homemade

Happy Birthday

How Does Your Garden Grow

How to Be a Fantastic Grandmother

Love & Friendship

Mom

Sisters

Tea Time Friends

The Gift of Friendship

They Call It Golf

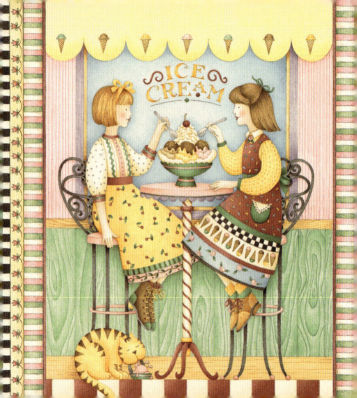

ICE
CREAM

✓ 1. Share a banana split at an old-fashioned ice cream parlor. Ask for two cherries so that you can each have "the cherry on top!"

crepe .

✓✓ 2. Have a slumber party. Go to an inn or bed and breakfast and have a girls' night out.

3. Check in daily with each other to offer support and encouragement and share laughter.

✓   4.   Take a craft class.

Make gifts for each other

and for your other friends.

5.   Attend a local community event

✓   such as a fair or a parade.

Be sure to share all treats like

cotton candy or caramel apples.

✓✓ 6. Share books, movies, ideas, philosophies, burdens, joys, and jokes.

✓ 7. Play games together–board games, card games, tennis, Frisbee.

✓✓ 8. Sing together with a song on the radio or even just a cappella.

9. Make buttery popcorn and watch a favorite movie together.

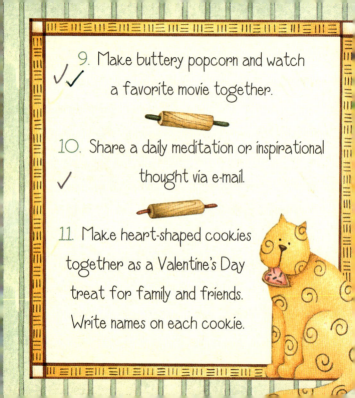

10. Share a daily meditation or inspirational thought via e-mail.

11. Make heart-shaped cookies together as a Valentine's Day treat for family and friends. Write names on each cookie.

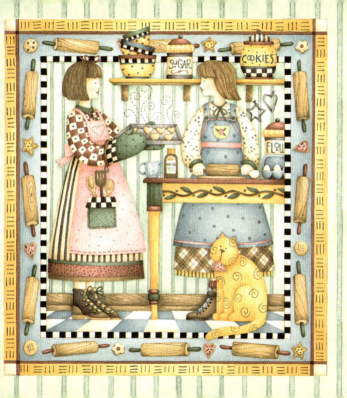

12. Have a girl's day out. Go shopping and to lunch (and, of course, enjoy a mid-afternoon chocolate snack).

13. Do what you can to help when your friend's in-laws are visiting.

14. Sign up for a charity walk-a-thon.
Make matching t-shirts
to identify your "team."

15. Put on your favorite music and dance
till you drop. The laughter will do you good.

✓ 16. Sit on the porch on a cool

summer evening in rocking chairs.

17. Go to a local nursing home

and adopt someone who has no family.

Let your families be their family.

✓ 18. Treat each other as irreplaceable. Take

care not to lose each other or your friendship.

✓ 19. Go to a free concert or play

at a local church or school.

20. Select a favorite quilt pattern and pool

your fabric to make matching friendship quilts.

✓ 21. Go on a nature walk. Bring your bird and wildflower field guides and keep a journal of birds and wildflowers that you identify.

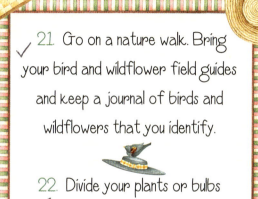

✓ 22. Divide your plants or bulbs and share your favorites with your friend.

23. Meet somewhere for coffee, ✓✓✓ dessert, and a nice long chat.

24. Home improvement projects go so much faster and are a lot more fun with a friend helping. Paint a room or work in the garden together—be sure to alternate projects at each other's homes!

½ ✓ 25. Join a book club together and attend a reading by an author at the local bookstore.

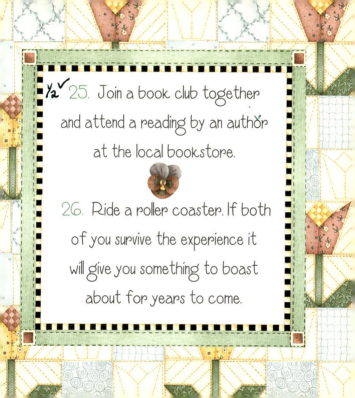

26. Ride a roller coaster. If both of you survive the experience it will give you something to boast about for years to come.

✓ 27. Get together to work on family scrapbooks or make your own friendship scrapbook with pictures and highlights of your time together.

✓ 28. Go to a department store for makeup makeovers. This is especially important near birthdays!

✓ 29. Have a clothes exchange.
Trade those outfits you never
wear. They'll feel new to
the other person.

✓ 30. Think of something really
silly you can do together and do it.
The memory will make you laugh.

31. Volunteer to help with Special Olympics.

✓ 32. Get together and wrap Christmas presents.

✓ 33. Go to a park and swing, slide, and ride the merry-go-round until all your troubles melt away.

✓ 34. Help each other decorate for the holidays. It makes any holiday twice as much fun.

35. Take your families to an orchard during a harvest festival. ✓ Then try your hand at making homemade jellies or preserves.

36. Visit sick friends or family together. Bring a feel-better gift such as homemade soup or a pampering kit with bath salts and lotion.

✓ 37. Be part of the committee that welcomes new members to your church or community.

✓ 38. Take a continuing education class that you will both enjoy.

39. Volunteer at a homeless shelter together.

40. Try on hats at a local
    department store.

41. Go to a concert by a favorite
    band from your high school days.
    Get matching t-shirts or hats.

42. Fly kites. If you and your friend
have children, fly kites with them. If you
    don't have children, borrow some.

✓✓ 43. Go on a trip together. Enjoy time away from your regular schedule.

✓ 44. Forget any minor annoyances. Remember all the kindnesses.

45. Have a family night. Get your
    families together for dinner
    and watch a movie you all like.

46. Never underestimate the joy
    of getting together for
    coffee in the morning.

47. Watch the Olympics together. Cheer for your favorite participants.

✓ 48. Go to a craft show together to buy presents and get decorating ideas.

49. If you have a disagreement, be the first to say, "I'm sorry."

√ 50. Honor each other's wishes. Don't force your own inclinations on your friend. For example, if she doesn't want a big birthday celebration, don't plan a big party.

✓ 51. Pack a picnic lunch for an
end-of-season picnic in a local park. Shuffle
through the leaves and find favorites
to take home for an autumn display.

✓ 52. Go to a circus.

✓ 53. Make special Christmas ornaments
and decorations for each other and for
other friends and family members.

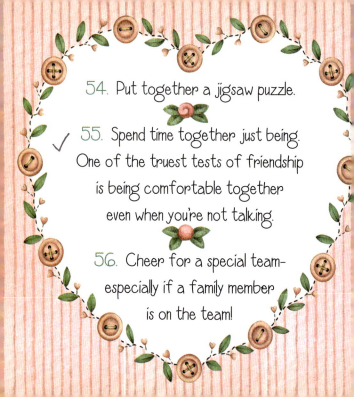

54. Put together a jigsaw puzzle.

55. Spend time together just being. One of the truest tests of friendship is being comfortable together even when you're not talking.

56. Cheer for a special team— especially if a family member is on the team!

57. Ride bikes through the neighborhood or on a bike trail.

58. Bundle up and go sledding or cross country skiing. Follow up with hot chocolate and plenty of marshmallows!

59. Visit a museum or historic neighborhood in your community.

60. Fix something. Even if you can't fix it, the experience is bound to make you laugh together.

61. National Friendship Day is the first Sunday in August. Plan something special for that day.

62. Leave funny messages
on each other's
answering machines. ✓ email

63. Keep one another's secrets.
Knowing you can trust someone
makes any friendship stronger.

64. Have an afternoon tea party at home or in your garden. Get out your best linens and china and make special treats.

65. Visit a public garden or conservatory to enjoy the beautiful flower displays.

✓ 66. Go antiquing. Stop at all the antique stores and junk shops that you've wondered about.

67. Take up a sport together and play on the same team.

68. Have your picture taken together. If there's a photo booth in your local mall, have several pictures taken. Be silly.

69. Give a party together. It will cut the work in half and double the fun.

✓ 70. Be truthful with each other gently. Remember telling the truth doesn't mean telling all you know.

71. Pick flowers in each other's gardens to press and use for future projects.

72. Head up the cheering section at your friend's special events. Always be her number one fan.

73. Go camping together. Sleeping outdoors and cooking over a fire is a great way to build memories.

74. Hug Often.

75. Celebrate your friendship every day.